D1530432

Muhammad

ALI

The Greatest

Written and Illustrated by Jim Spence

THE ROURKE PRESS, INC.
VERO BEACH, FL 32964

Edited by Sandra A. Robinson and Pamela J.P. Schroeder

LIBRARY OF CONGRESS CATALOGING-IN-PUBLICATION DATA

Spence, Jim
    Muhammad Ali, the greatest / written and illustrated by Jim Spence.
        p.   cm. — (Great comeback champions)
    Summary: Relates the events which led a child victim of a stolen bike to become the only man in boxing history to win the Heavyweight Title three times.
    ISBN 1-57103-005-0
    1. Ali, Muhammad, 1942-   —Juvenile literature. 2. Boxers (Sports)— United States—Biography—Juvenile literature. [1. Ali, Muhammad, 1942-   . 2. Boxers (Sports) 3. Afro-Americans—Biography.] I. Title. II. Series: Spence, Jim. Great comeback champions.
GV1132.A44S64   1995
796.8'3'092—dc20
[B]   95-5360
                                                                                           CIP
                                                                                            AC

Printed in the USA

"Ladies and gentlemen, introducing the new
Heavyweight Champion of the World, Cassius Clay!"
shouts the ring announcer.

This is the story of the most exciting and colorful
athlete in the history of boxing—Cassius Clay—today
known as, Muhammad Ali.

Starting Out

"Please, officer, can you help me?" asked young Cassius. "Someone has stolen my new bike!" The officer was Joe Martin. He was able to help Cassius, but in a surprising way.

Joe was in charge of a local boxing gym in Louisville, Kentucky. He talked with Cassius about learning to box so he could defend himself against the bigger boys who had stolen his bike.

Cassius liked the idea and became more and more interested in boxing. Each day he would rush down to the gym after school to practice his skills. When Cassius told his parents that he wanted to make boxing his career, they supported him. They had faith in him and believed he could be an excellent boxer if he worked hard.

After graduating from high school in 1960, Cassius earned a place on the United States Olympic boxing team. His parents were very proud that he was representing their country.

Cassius promised a gold medal victory—and he delivered it by defeating Zbigniew Pietrzykowski of Poland. Now Cassius Clay was ready to step in the ring of professional boxing.

Turning Pro

Cassius Clay amazed everyone when he won his first 19 professional fights in a row—15 by knockouts! What came next was every boxer's dream—a chance to win the Heavyweight Crown.

On February 25, 1964, when he was only 22, Cassius Clay fought Sonny Liston for the Heavyweight Title of the World. Most of the experts believed Liston would win, because he had more experience. Sonny was a brawler, a fighter who was rough and tough. On the other hand, at 6 feet, 3 inches tall and weighing in at 220 pounds, Cassius had amazing quickness in his feet and lightning-fast hands.

Before the fight Cassius boldly predicted, "I'll float like a butterfly and sting like a bee"—and he did just that! He won in the sixth round over Liston to take the Heavyweight Title. His words echoed throughout the world, "I am the *greatest!*"

Standing Up for His Beliefs

Soon after winning the Heavyweight Title of the World, Cassius Clay became a member of the Black Muslim faith and changed his name to Muhammad Ali. Because of his religious beliefs, Muhammad Ali refused to be drafted by the United States military.

As a result, in 1967, Ali was banned from boxing. Though some people were angry at Ali for standing up for his beliefs, many people thought he had courage.

In 1970, the Supreme Court ruled that Ali should no longer be banned from the sport he loved. The boxer was once again ready to step into the ring.

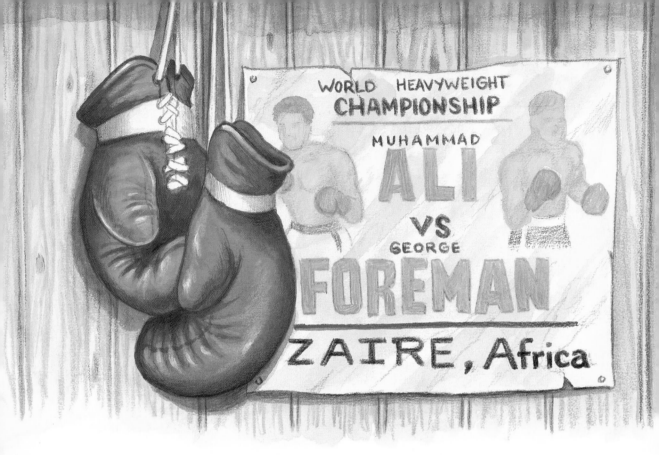

Meeting New Challenges

In 1974, in Zaire, Africa, Ali met his biggest challenge—reigning Heavyweight Champion George Foreman.

The press and many sports fans did not think Ali had a chance to win. After all, he hadn't boxed professionally for three and a half years. However, Ali outsmarted everyone when he used a tactic he named "Rope a Dope."

Ali leaned against the ropes and covered his face
and body with his arms. Foreman could not hit Ali's
chest, stomach or head, and that made him mad.
George began to punch harder and harder until his
arms became tired. When he could barely lift them,
Ali was ready to attack. He shocked the world by
knocking out the powerful Foreman. Ali had won the
Heavyweight Title for the second time.

Perhaps Ali's most famous fights were with Joe Frazier. Joe was a good match for Ali, both in and out of the ring. Months before their fights took place, the two often appeared in TV interviews, taunting and joking about each other. The fans loved the pre-fight rivalry and Ali and Joe Frazier were very popular.

Ali and Frazier's third match was fought on October 1, 1975, in Manilla, Philippines. The "Thrilla in Manilla" was perhaps the greatest Heavyweight Championship ever fought. Ali held on to win and remain the champion.

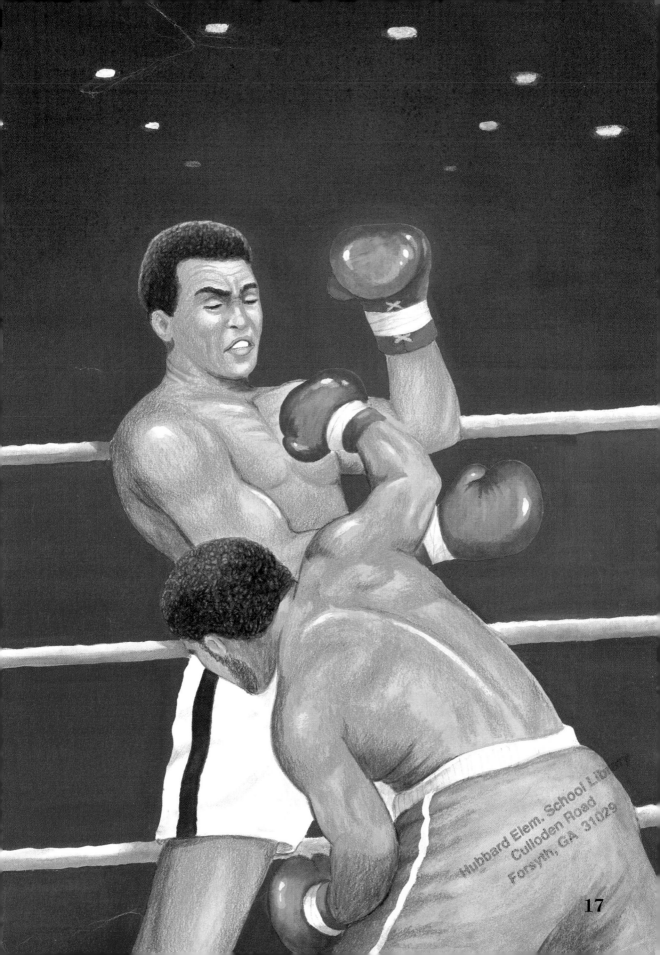

17

18

Reaching Out

Muhammad Ali is the only man in the history of boxing to win the Heavyweight Title three times.

Today his challenges are different. Since his retirement, Ali has suffered from a disorder of the nervous system known as Parkinson's disease. He is still active in missionary work and often makes public appearances. People throughout the world love and respect Muhammad Ali.

"Ali is the greatest fighter that I have ever worked for," claims longtime trainer and friend Angelo Dundee. "To me, he is dynamite."

Muhammad
ALI

TIMELINE AND TRIUMPHS

1942   Born January 17 in Louisville, Kentucky

1959-60   National Golden Gloves Light Heavyweight
Champion

1959-60   National Amateur Athletic Union Light
Heavyweight Champion

1960   U.S. Olympic Gold Medalist

1960   Kentucky Golden Gloves Light Heavyweight
Champion

1964   Heavyweight Champion of the World
defeating Sonny Liston (seventh-round
technical knockout)

1971   Lost Heavyweight Title to Joe Frazier
(15th-round decision)

1974   Defeated George Foreman, became
Heavyweight Champion for the second time
(eighth-round knockout)

1978 Lost Heavyweight Title to Leon Spinks (15th-round decision)

1978 Regained Heavyweight Title defeating Leon Spinks (15th-round decision)

1983 Honored in U.S. Olympic Hall of Fame

1990 Honored in International Boxing Hall of Fame

★ Only boxer in history to win Heavyweight Title three times

★ In 61 fights, Ali won 56 times—37 by knockouts

GREAT COMEBACK CHAMPIONS

ARTHUR ASHE
Tennis Legend

BO JACKSON
Super Athlete

JOE MONTANA
The Comeback Kid

JULIE KRONE
Fearless Jockey

MUHAMMAD ALI
The Greatest

NANCY KERRIGAN
Courageous Skater